How To Have
"Unexpected" Income!

John Wolcott Adams

Published by Golden Key Publications
P. O. Box 13367
Scottsdale, AZ 85267-3356 USA

How to Have "Unexpected" Income

Other books by John Wolcott Adams

Be What You Are: Love
Power Words for Prosperous Living!
Thirty Days to a Better Life
Positively Alive!

Cassette Tapes by the Author:
Money is Wonderful!
A Two-Cassette Album

How to Demonstrate Abundant Prosperity

Prosperous Living Power
200 Affirmations from the book:
Power Words for Prosperous Living!

First Printing, January, 1995

ISBN-9602166-7-7

Printed in UNITES STATES OF AMERICA
by Publishers Press
Salt Lake City, Utah

Contents . . .

It is your Father's good pleasure to give you His treasure in Marvelous Measure!

This book is lovingly dedicated
to "Beautiful Sunshine."

Introduction . . . .

What this book will do for you . . .
A personal note from the author.

This book is for prosperity-loving people and is the culmination of many years of sharing prospering ideas with readers of my newsletter. Thousands of people who have applied them in their daily lives continue to enjoy the financial and other rich good that comes to them through the teaching of these concepts. Because of their success, as well as my own, I know that you too, can reap exciting rewards by following the instructions in this book. Use the Prayer-Treatment for "unexpected" income and get ready for happy results!

The purpose of this book is to help you open your mind, accept, and enjoy the exciting "extra" money and all of the rich blessings available to you through the practice of expecting "unexpected" income! Through the teachings presented here, you will learn of the vast possibilities for unlimited financial income, and all kinds of good available to you. You'll learn how to raise your monetary supply to a more satisfying level.

This book is intended to help you expand your thinking and awareness of the unlimited good that is waiting for you. Thus you may claim and experience all of the happiness, good health, love, peace, and prosperity God intends for you. He wants you to enjoy it all now!

Unfortunately, many people do not give sufficient thought to being as prosperous as they could and have a right to be. While giving thought to being "religious" they often fail to see the connection between spirituality and prosperity; the two are divinely connected. Therefore, they deny themselves much of the joy and prosperity that are theirs by divine right.

A basic reason that more people do not enjoy more money and what it can provide is that they *look only to one or two avenues (job, etc.) for their financial supply.* By thinking in this limited way, they may also hold beliefs about themselves as being unworthy and therefore cannot not expect to have much. Consequently, they believe that they need not give much time or energy to the obtaining of money.

Through their unenlightened thinking, they create a consciousness of limitation rather than one of personal abundance. They fail to look beyond the usual ways in which their good comes to them. *Unexpected Income* enables you to overcome limited thinking. It empowers you to free up the channels of your financial supply, at the same time expanding your reasoning in relation to the supply itself.

If you haven't done so lately, begin now to ponder the vastness of universal supply--it is yours for the asking, claiming and accepting when you do the right things. Deliberately stretch your thinking out of the circumscribed and habitual thought-patterns that have created your present financial condition. Of course, your present financial condition may be pretty good; you may even be a millionaire! That's great--but, *you can always do better.*

Determine that you will exercise your mind in such a way that will result in much larger images regarding the availability of universal substance which will prospers you.

Decide to lift your faith and use your imagination to perceive that which you want. Visualize the increased good actually manifesting for you. Accept that it is probably doing so right now without reservation or limitation.

Since the only blocks to unlimited financial supply are in the individual's thinking, by removing the self-imposed limits, you unlimit your financial supply, as well as all the other wonderful blessings possible for you.

Your belief system makes you rich or poor, or somewhere in between. To raise your level of prosperity, there must be an appropriate adjustment in your belief system.

As you make that adjustment, not only do you receive happy financial "surprises," you'll have more confidence, and the struggle and striving for financial gain will fade away. In fact, you may become so excited about this efficient and pleasant way of increasing your financial supply, you'll wish you had found it sooner!

Best of all, you will become a believer! You will know, beyond a doubt, that you have a "Divine Connection"* with the Source of all wealth that never runs dry. Your prosperity dreams start coming true and you will enjoy ever-increasing prosperity in your daily life.

To learn more about your "Divine Connection", refer to the author's book, "Power Words For Prosperous Living."

How to Have "Unexpected" Income is the result of many years of working with prosperous-thinking people, sharing with them the exciting "unexpected" income concept, and helping them to learn and apply the dynamic laws of prosperity so they too could create lives of true abundance.

My desire in sharing the "unexpected" income idea with my readers is for you to learn and use this practical and fun way to increase your financial income so you may experience more of the riches to which you are entitled. I want you to experience *prosperous living* at its finest!

Now, open your mind to "unexpected" income and read this book in anticipation of the wonderful things that may happening to you. As you read the accounts of "unexpected" income, you'll be convinced of the efficacy of this practice. You will join the many thousands of people worldwide who are already increasing their financial wealth through learning *How to have "unexpected" income!*

Do not be surprised if within a few days of reading this book (or perhaps while still reading it), some financial "surprises" come to you. Good things often begin to happen when you open your mind to "unexpected" income! Watch for them because they will surely come.

You will discover that this is a practical and empowering prosperity book in that it will enable you to raise your prosperity to a higher level-- and have fun doing it!

The Universe wants you to have MORE! You deserve more of all that makes life happier, healthier, fulfilling and beautiful. Go ahead; claim and accept all of the rich good that is yours by divine right as the beloved child of a fabulously rich Universe. *Go for it with all your heart!*

John Wolcott Adams
P. O. Box 13356
Scottsdale, AZ 85267 USA

1

You Can Cause a Flow of Financial Abundance in Your Life!

You would, I am sure, be happy and excited if you unexpectedly received some extra money, even a relatively small amount. If it were a large sum, you'd probably get very excited! Possibly you have already had that great feeling and would like to have it more often. You can!

You can develop a habit of receiving wonderful and happy financial "surprises" on a regular basis, and cause more and more money to come into your life. You can experience such an inflow of financial substance that it will amaze you and make your life happier as well as more prosperous.

Russell H. Conwell, said in his famous *Acres of Diamonds lecture:* "You ought to be rich; you have no right to be poor." In other words, it is okay for you to be rich, but poor is unacceptable.

The primary way for you to create a flow of financial abundance in your life--to enjoy "unexpected" income--is to use the special Prayer-Treatment for "unexpected" income which you will find on pages 20 and 21. Thousands of people worldwide use it with excellent results. They are enjoying the happy financial "surprises" that come through cooperating with the prospering law. Some results may seem small, but each one is important and raises your level of expectancy.

A person in Indiana wrote: "I thank God for a fantastic $122.00 'unexpected' income blessing. I received a letter some months ago from a company for which I had worked nine years earlier. The letter stated that they owed me $122.00 and would be sending that amount to me. I soon forgot about the letter. Then, one day I receive a check for $122.00. What a miracle! I believe you'll be hearing from me again real soon! I am so grateful for past blessing, this blessing, and for all that are on the way to me now. Thank you for sharing the 'unexpected' income idea with me."

How to Have "Unexpected" Income

A lady in Illinois reported: "I received a portable refrigerator. My daughter sent a check to me which paid for my doctor visit. Also, I received unexpected cash in amounts of $5.00, $20.00, and $45.00."

From Wyoming: "Since I began using the Prayer-Treatment for 'unexpected' income, I have received a check for dental insurance in the amount of $480.00, and I was made supervisor at $12.00 per hour, increased from $9.50 per hour that I was receiving. Also, I received a totally unexpected check in the amount of $60.00. I am a believer!"

An "unexpected" income report from Idaho: "On the day I received my 'unexpected' income information, a friend gave me $50.00 from money she had received unexpectedly. Three days later, an out-of-town visitor gave me $40.00. Just yesterday a friend gave me $150.00 and today I got a job!"

Referring client brings "unexpected" Income: "I referred a customer to a broker and did not expect to be rewarded so much ($500.00), and it came just before Christmas. Thank you for this great idea. It is working beautifully for me."
                                    - - *From California*

Another Californian reported: "I recently received $700.00 in 'unexpected' Income. I want to express my appreciation for such a fine program. It really works!"

From a New Yorker: "Since joining the 'unexpected' income activity and using the Prayer-Treatment as instructed, I have received approximately $225.00. I thank God for this, and for such a fun way to increase my income. I have no doubt that my financial blessings will continue. I am so grateful for all the other people who are blessing me while using the Prayer-Treatment. I am blessing others each day, too."

These people began receiving when they opened their minds to "unexpected" income and used the Prayer-Treatment daily as instructed. In so doing, they began to clear away limitations which had held them captive to restricted financial supply. In addition, they no longer limited the avenues through which their financial supply could come.

It's just as easy for you too!

Everyone loves surprises, especially money or something as good. Surprises are exciting and fun; the element of surprise doubles the pleasure. It can be easy for you to receive "unexpected" income too. Beside it is right for you to do so.

You can cause "unexpected" income to manifest in your life regularly. There is a way to make it a happy habit, and that is through your own thinking. The secret is to create within your thinking the *expectancy* of extra money.

When you do the right thing, hold the right thoughts, and use dynamic prosperity principles, you are sure to experience "unexpected" financial gain.

An Irresistible Magnet

As you use the Prayer-Treatment for "unexpected" income, a positive vibration radiates from you that transforms you into an irresistible magnet for wonderful happenings. You literally set yourself up for one positive experience after another. Life becomes an exciting adventure and you will expect good things to happen. Best of all, they do!

The golden key to that kind of life is in using your wonderful mind as God intends--to create a happy, healthy, peaceful and financially secure life full of love, joy, and wonder! Your thinking has *everything* to do with what you experience. Using the Prayer-Treatment for "unexpected" income establishes a force-field that attracts to you more and more positive experiences.

A good thought to keep in mind is: *Everything that comes TO you comes THROUGH you.*

When you understand that you are the main channel through which your good comes, and you are wise enough to do what is right, you will cooperate with prosperity laws and principles. You will then do whatever is necessary to establish yourself in the mental and physical environment that is financially productive and satisfying for you. *Prosperous thinking produces prosperous living!*

Remember, it is love that fulfills your desires. When love is the foundation of all that you do, you and everyone benefits.

*Love is by far
the most important thing
of all.*

2

Not a Get-Rich-Quick Scheme

The "Unexpected" income idea is not a get-rich-quick scheme. Nor is it an overnight financial success plan--although it may very well trigger such a flow of money in your life you will think you have hit the "mother lode!" On the other hand, it may not produce fabulous wealth but help you to be more financially comfortable. It's really up to you.

If you expect to "come into sudden wealth," you may be disappointed, but if you will begin and persist in faithfully using the Prayer-Treatment for "unexpected" income, you are likely to have some exciting money-demonstrations right away.

As you continue to use the concepts daily, thus establishing the practice as a habit, the demonstrations will occur on a regular basis. That's a nice habit to have!

So-called get-rich-quick schemes do not usually work. Rather, they more often leave the participants poorer than before. Such schemes are for gullible people who are usually looking for a quick fix for a life of meager financial existence, which is born of the belief that one must struggle just to get by. They are people who are looking for an easy way to get rich without using their minds to think prosperously first. Neither do they make a sincere effort to gain financially through means in accord with the laws and principles of prosperity.

Examples of *get-rich-quick* schemes are chain-letters and similar inducements usually sent through the mail. Not only are they illegal, they don't work. They don't work because they violate spiritual law. They're a waste of time, money, and energy. Regardless of what is stated in chain-letters--and I've seen hundreds of them --it simply isn't true. Use your mind and your money more wisely!

Another concept that does not work, except temporarily and for a very few people, is the pyramid scheme. This is when large sums of money are passed around in the belief that everyone who participates will receive thousands of dollars in a relatively short time. Pyramids are also in violation of a basic spiritual law: *You cannot get something for nothing.*

In stating that "unexpected" income is not a *get-rich-quick* scheme, it is necessary to point out, that it is *not a scheme at all.* As I have already stated, it is not something by which you will suddenly come into wealth. However, I want to quickly add: You *will* begin to experience some pleasant financial surprises.. Some of these may come quickly; others will take a little longer. The most important benefit is the creating of Prosperity Consciousness out of which is manifested financial and other good forms of wealth. "Unexpected" income helps you do that.

"Unexpected" income is based upon sound prosperity laws and principles while *get-rich-quick* schemes are not. Your goal should be not only for your financial income to be permanent, but to increase as well.   That can only be accomplished through building it upon universal prosperity laws and principles.

It doesn't cost anything to become involved in "unexpected" income--except for the cost of this book which just may turn out to be a small investment that pays great dividends.

You have every right to adopt and use this easy method for increasing what you so well deserve: *Larger, ever-increasing and more satisfying financial supply.* Pay no attention to what others may say. No matter who might doubt the effectiveness of this prospering activity, it will work well when you exercise full faith. Just go ahead and reap the prosperous results.

"Unexpected" income is not something that happens *outside* yourself as much as it is something that occurs *within* you. It begins in your mind and your thinking is the channel through which it comes. It is essential to understand and accept this. The more you practice this prospering principle, the better it will work. Make it part of your daily activity.

In other words, you create your prosperity in your own belief system first. As you do this, happy financial "surprises" and other good things will come to you. You will get up in the morning expecting the "unexpected." You will go to sleep at night, thankful for a day in which the "unexpected" did in deed happen; good things --financial and otherwise--came to you!

"Unexpected" income works for you as you begin to cooperate with spiritual laws and principles, and allow yourself to be an open and free instrument through which the Universe pours out the unlimited good It has for you.

"Unexpected" income is a bonafied, mental and spiritual activity that results in increased financial supply for those who faithfully participate--in other words "unexpected" income.

You can begin now to bring

prosperity into your home.

The first thing for you to do is to

discard the words that have in them

the idea of poverty, and then select

carefully the words that hold

the idea of plenty.

-- Myrtle Fillmore

3

Prayer-Treatment for "Unexpected" Income

On the next two pages is the Prayer-Treatment for "Unexpected" income which has been used successfully for many years by thousands of prosperity-loving people. Following the Prayer-Treatment, you will find a detailed explanation of what a Prayer-Treatment is and how to use it. Please read the Prayer-Treatment through. If it is new to you, you will immediately begin to realize the power of it. If you have used it before, you will be familiar with its effectiveness for bringing happy, prospering results. Either way it works beautifully for those who faithfully use it on a daily basis.

For best results, use the Prayer-Treatment once or twice each day.

Prayer-Treatment for "Unexpected" Income.

I believe God is the Source of all supply, and Money is God in action and should be used for good.

I believe my good is now freely flowing to me so bountifully I cannot use it all, and I have an abundance to spare and share today, and always.

I am expecting "unexpected" income!

I believe God is giving to me now and I accept this as Truth and give thanks.

All channels of financial supply are open to me now and I am richly, bountifully, and beautifully prospered in every good way.

I believe true prosperity includes the demonstration of right living conditions, right activity and genuine happiness.

This word which I speak in faith believing activates the Law of INCREASED universal good for me, and I EXPECT to see rich results now!

I visualize the financial good I expect. I see it coming to me now, richly and abundantly.

I claim and accept it for myself now.

I am grateful in advance! I bless all the good I have now, and I bless the increase.

I bless all others who are using this Prayer-Treatment for "unexpected" income. I KNOW we are ALL prospering together in every good way, and we share the good we receive.

I now freely give my tenth to God's good work. My giving makes me rich!

God gives to me rich, lavish, happy financial blessings now!

This is so now. I am grateful. Thank You, Father!

*A Spiritual Treatment is
a change of mind.
When the mind changes,
the outer expression must change
to correspond, indeed,
Paul says,
"We are transformed by the
renewing of our minds."*
-- Emmet Fox

4

What is
Prayer-Treatment?

Prayer and Treatment mean more or less the same thing. Whether you say, Prayer or Treatment or Prayer-Treatment, you are invoking universal spiritual power for good. This should not be confused with beseeching or begging for something, because it is already yours.

Prayer-Treatment is affirming that which is true regardless of appearances, and in spite of the fact that your declaration may not seem to be true. When you use Prayer-Treatment, which is scientific prayer, you are expanding your belief system in order to incorporate prosperity-producing ideas. In other words, you are changing your mind for the better. When your thinking changes, the outer expression changes accordingly.

Change occurs when you have convinced your subconscious mind that something is true. Since the subconscious mind directly communicates with Superconscious Mind, the wheels are set in motion, so-to-speak, for universal substance to bring prosperity.

Thus, it is through the Superconscious Mind that universal substance is poured into the mold that you create with your imagination and faith.

Prayer-Treatment empowers you to experience what you truly desire. It is different, however, than random thinking and speaking. Specific prayer-treatment gives definite, positive direction to your thought process. It provides direct contact with universal substance which is always at hand, waiting as it were, to manifest according to your thoughts and spoken word.

Speaking audibly is best because it gives the Prayer-Treatment more power and makes a greater impact upon your mind. Sometimes it may be necessary to repeat the same words over and over until the impression is made on your subconscious mind, or until a definite change has occurred. However, do not under-estimate the power of "speaking" the words silently as well; meditating on them has power, too.

While using a prayer-treatment for any purpose, allow yourself to recognize Universal Substance's omniscience, omnipotence, and omnipresence, and that you are inseparably unified with It. When you do this, you will be greatly empowered. Nothing is impossible to you because you will make of yourself a willing instrument through which Spiritual Substance has an open channel for expressing Its good.

Prayer-Treatment is a highly spiritualized activity of the mind in which you conceive, realize, and accept inner peace, poise, power, and the abundance of happiness, health, and success according to your desires. In this spiritual activity, you practice the presence of God, and in so doing, mentally connect with the Source. This is mightily important in demonstrating your desired good.

There is no limit to what you may realize and demonstrate. If the Prayer-Treatment idea is new to you, please do not reject it out-of-hand. Rather, act in faith and be amazed at how easily it works if you persist.

The next chapter gives you instruction for using the Prayer-Treatment for demonstrating "unexpected" income.

For best results, follow these instructions prayerfully to have the joy of experiencing desired results. As someone once said, "When nothing else works, "read the directions." Chapter Five gives directions so as to maximize the potential of "unexpected" income for you.

If, for some reason, you don't demonstrate prosperity to your satisfaction, re-read chapter five to refresh your mind. It is not hard to receive "unexpected" income; the most important requirement is faith. Exercise it!

5

Instruction for Using the Prayer-Treatment

For best results, do these things:

1. Use the Prayer-Treatment for "unexpected" income every day, beginning now.

When I say "use", I mean speak the words of the Treatment. Reading the treatment silently is powerful in itself, but there is much more energy released by affirming the words aloud.

The words you speak set up a vibration that goes out into the furthest reaches of the Universe and makes a definite impact upon divine substance. That substance will in turn respond and come to you in the form of your declaration.

Do not under-estimate the power of your spoken word. There is great power in the words you speak, so make sure they are harmonious with what you want to achieve. For more information on the spoken word, please refer to the author's book, *Power Words for Prosperous Living!*

2. Use the Prayer-Treatment at least once or twice daily.

Once or twice should be sufficient. You do not want to overexert, which implies lack of faith. Rather, speak these words of Truth in the assurance that what you declare is so. It is! Affirm and let it go!

However, daily use of the Prayer-Treatment is essential to create the steady flow of money and other good things that will come to you. Approach this activity exactly as you would with anything that you really want to experience. The more important it is to you, the more enthusiastic you will be. Enthusiasm is success-energy!

You may want to use the Prayer-Treatment in the morning and again before going to sleep at night. However, just once each day will bring good results; do what works best for you.

3. Sincerely desire "unexpected" income for everyone who is using the Prayer-Treatment.

Remember that there are thousands of people using this Prayer-Treatment each day. Like you, they desire "unexpected" income for themselves, but they are also desiring it for you. Thus, tremendous prospering power is generated that benefits everyone. One can only imagine how much prospering energy is flowing because of everyone's activity. In addition, be assured that it also has a definite positive impact upon the whole planet.

As you are open and receptive and audibly declaring the Prayer-Treatment, you are at the same time backed up--so-to-speak--by many other people who are doing the same. You may not know each other, but that doesn't matter. Infinite Intelligence knows each of you and is in everyone, seeing to it that all prosper. *We are all in it together!*

Sincerely desiring the same for others demonstrates complete unselfishness and helps you prosper even as others do. There is more than enough for everyone! This practice is a great way to spread around God's good green energy called money!

4. Have faith.

Hold your faith and expectations high. BELIEVE YOU RECEIVE. It is according to your faith that it is done unto you. You cannot expect this or anything else to work for you unless you put your complete faith and trust in it.

When you do, you *know* that you are receiving "unexpected" income NOW and cannot do otherwise. Your faith goes before you, opening out the way for all manner of rich blessings to come to you. Through your faith, you cause universal "gold dust" to settle upon you and your life.

5. Put God first financially.

Give your tithe (10%)* of all you receive back to God, the Source of your rich supply. Do so without fail, and do it first. It is an essential part of demonstrating "unexpected" income. If you have not been tithing, perhaps due to struggling financially, tithing will help to eliminate the struggle. Furthermore, it will empower you to be richer in *every* possible way. *Tithing will be explained more fully in Chapter Twelve..*

6. Open your mind to every possibility.

Look to God for your supply. Do NOT limit the number of channels through which His abundance may come to you. His channels are infinite, just as His supply is unlimited also.

Since God is within you, your supply must always be where you are. So open your mind wide; expand your horizons until you have a larger view of what you may have been missing out on. There are many wonderful "surprises" in store for you.

Because abundance is unlimited, it can never run out. You owe it to yourself to let go of old, limited ways of thinking and claim more of the good God has for you.

7. Accept.

God gives according to your acceptance, so --ACCEPT! Above all, do it with gratitude!

You may pray and pray for riches, but it is only through your ability to *accept* the good that the Infinite can give it to you. When you sit at a banquet table, and you can have whatever you are willing to partake of, what you receive is up to you.

31

In other words, you can receive only that which you allow yourself to accept. Acceptance with gratitude clears the way for a continuing stream of "unexpected" income in many forms!

The "Gratitude Attitude" is your "Open Sesame" to universal riches. It is through the thankful heart that the Universe loves to pour Its vast wealth. *(The "Gratitude Attitude" is covered more thoroughly in Chapter Thirteen.)*

8. Persist.

As with everything else, there is real success power in persistence.

It has been rightly said that persistence alone will propel one to success, fame and fortune when everything else seems to fail. By doggedly keeping on in faith believing, you *will* win.

People sometimes seem to tire of using the Prayer-treatment, or their faith falters. This is when they allow old, limiting belief systems be in control. Thus, they keep themselves from experiencing the abundance they could have very well had by persevering.

Therefore, persist by affirming the Prayer-Treatment *every day.* It is also helpful to meditate upon it silently as you allow the truths it contains to quietly find a welcomed resting place within. In so doing, you will empower yourself to experience those wonderful "surprises" that are sure to start appearing in your life.

9. Give.

Giving begets receiving. As you give, it is given unto you. You should not expect to receive something for nothing. Giving primes the pump and gets the flow going. *(More on giving is presented in Chapter Twelve.)*

10. Be happy! Be Optimistic! Put plenty of love and joy into all you do.

Determine that you will be just as happy as though you have won the lottery or are already receiving one financial blessing after another. Instead of focusing upon appearances of lack, concentrate on the wonderful good that is on its way to you now.

Joy opens the mind and clears the way for God's rich good to be expressed and manifested through you. Joy is love expressing. Love creates in you an irresistible magnet that attracts God's best to you.

As you speak the Prayer-Treatment, do it happily and joyfully, allowing love to well up within you. Where you are right now, feel love for God's good, ready and manifesting in your life and affairs.

Along with the words you are speaking for others, send them love. You may not know any of them, but love and bless them anyway. Accept that they are doing the same for you and return it to them. It comes back "pressed down and running over."

Acting in love completes the circuit and keeps divine substance moving. Concern for the well-being of others is the very substance of love, and love is the power that moves substance into your life. Love expressed in joy and optimism brings prospering results!

Please see the author's book, "BE What You Are: LOVE" for more on the prospering power of Love.)

The Prayer-Treatment for "Unexpected" Income Explained

The following six chapters will give you a deeper look into each declaration of the Prayer-Treatment in order to expand your understanding.

Increasing your understanding of the principles gives more substance to your faith, thus empowering you to more successfully experience "unexpected" income. Augmenting your faith opens the way for you to reap a more abundant harvest of the blessings that you want to receive.

At the very least, these chapters will help you move toward understanding the Prayer-Treatment by creating a strong positive signal that will radiate from you and attract "unexpected" income.

How much can we demonstrate?
Just what one can believe.
How much can we see,
how much can we accept,
how much can we find in
our consciousness that is no
longer repudiated by denials?
What ever that is,
that much we can have.
                              -- Ernest Holmes

6

God is the Source

I believe God is the source of all supply, and Money is God in action, and should be used for good.

First of all, what you believe is of utmost importance because it has everything to do with what manifests in your life. Therefore, it is essential that you believe that God is the Source of *all* supply, and in particular *your* supply.

If you want to demonstrate abundance, you must acknowledge God as the one and only source. Although it appears that money comes through jobs, the government, securities, and other avenues, these are not the Source, but only *channels* through which your financial supply manifests.

You may severely limit your supply if you look only to channels instead of to God, the Source.

A young man had a very good job that he liked and which paid well. He thought he was secure for life as long as he did his work and kept everything in perspective. When the company suddenly began cutting back, he became frightened, and sure enough his turn came to be laid off.

For a while he was bitter, blaming the company; then one day, he was given a book on *prosperous living*. As he began to read, he learned why he had been laid off. It wasn't because the company no longer needed him, but that he needed to learn that God is the Source of his supply.

Thus the young man learned to go directly to the Source, through prayer and meditation. With this activity, he learned to incorporate the dynamic laws and principles of prosperity into his thinking, never doubting that God is the Source of his supply. Moreover, he learned that God is a very loving, all-providing Presence always with him, ready to give to him whatever he desires.

The right way to express the desire, of course, is through affirmative prayer. He declared over and over:

GOD IS MY SOURCE, THEREFORE, MY SUPPLY IS WHERE I AM AND I AM ALWAYS ABUNDANTLY PROVIDED FOR.

As he continued in this new way of thinking he soon secured employment with a company that offered him more money than he was earning before. This time, he kept the thought uppermost in his mind: *God is the Source and my supply.* Each day through prayer and meditation, he dwelt consciously in the Presence, acknowledging that God is the all-providing, never-failing Source of his supply.

Further more, as he progressed, he came to the realization that the Source can never run dry. An important part of his development came through learning the prosperity law of tithing. He then made an agreement with God to faithfully give back at least ten per cent of all that he received.

Actually, losing his job turned out to be a blessing for this young man in that it caused him to search within himself and discover the vast riches of universal supply.

Through affirmative prayer and his belief in God as the Source of his supply, he went on to create a satisfying life for himself that included a lovely, supportive wife, children, and the home of their dreams.

Money is God in action. If you have been taught that money is evil and acquiring it should be avoided, think about it. Money will enable you to go places you cannot go and do things you cannot do without it.

Since God is everywhere present, that means that God is in everything. His substance is the "stuff" out of which everything is made. There is nothing but this ONE SUBSTANCE! God is only good and money is a manifestation of God's Substance, therefore MONEY HAS TO BE GOOD. The truth is, *Money is wonderful!*

Because money is a medium of exchange it is always moving. Money constantly changes hands in the form of cash, checks, credit cards, or in other forms. Although it may not be readily detected, an incredible amount of money is continually on the move!

If money is God in action, then it is God Who is constantly moving money and causing all manner of good things to happen!

Some people use money for less than honorable purposes; make sure that money which comes to you is used for only that which is good. Determine that your behavior and use of money will not harm anyone but will add to their good.

Using money only for good is in keeping with the dynamic laws of prosperity. It is love in action and will assure that only good will continue to come to you. Using money in the highest and best ways creates activity that blesses you and countless other people, too. Thus, the world is made a better place for everyone.

(For more on the goodness of money, see the author's books, "BE What You Are: LOVE." and "Power Words for Prosperous Living!," and Cassette album: entitled "Money is Wonderful!")

I believe my good is now freely flowing to me so bountifully I cannot use it all, and I have an abundance to spare and share, today and always.

Here again, belief is important. Check up on what *you* believe about *your* good. Believe that your good is flowing freely. Not only is it flowing freely but so bountifully that you cannot possibly use it all. It is coming in such overflowing abundance it can never run out. What a wonderful thought! If, on the other hand, that does not seem to be happening, what--or *who*--could be stopping it?

Please do not think that I am talking about being greedy--far from it! In the first place, you are seeking to demonstrate for yourself only that which you want for everyone else as well. Secondly, it is right for you to have plenty. More than enough is far better than never having enough--always scraping and struggling to take care of financial obligations. When you have more than you need rather than not enough, there is plenty to share and sharing will bring peace of mind to you and others as well.

There is something wonderful about sharing. Those with whom you share are blessed, but giving leads to receiving and more will come back to you also. It creates a wonderful circle of divine activity--God's way of moving His infinite riches around. It is God, as well as money, in action.

So, believe that your good--your rich supply --is always flowing so freely and bountifully that you cannot use it all. Declare and accept that you always have a rich abundance to spare and share.

I am expecting "Unexpected" Income.

You may think that since you are using the Prayer-Treatment and especially if you are *expecting* to be financially blessed, then it is not really *unexpected* income.

However, even though you expect it, the manner in which it comes is *unexpected.* You need not be concerned with HOW it is coming but believe and expect that it will. When you declare the Prayer-Treatment affirmations, universal substance will work for you, and you have *every* right to expect financial and other wonderful "surprises" to come to you.

A person in Louisiana wrote: "I have been faithfully using the Prayer-Treatment for 'unexpected' income. At my husband's company, vacations are in full swing and they are understaffed. Because of this, he was asked to work two extra shifts which, of course, resulted in extra income which was unexpected.

"Today, I purchased two needed items on sale. I saved $5.00 on one item and $17.00 on others. There is something special about using the Prayer-Treatment in that it causes me to *expect* money and other good things to come to me, but somehow it is always surprising when they do. It does help to have an attitude of positive expectancy. I *know* it is coming but I never know *how* it is going to come--amazing!"

7

Accept It Now

I believe God is giving this to me now and I accept this as Truth and give thanks.

As always, belief plays an important part in the achieving of good results. Having established that God is the Source of all supply including *yours*, it is essential to believe that God, the Source, is giving to you what you ask for and in the form of your desires.

It is also important to affirm and accept that God is giving it to YOU. While you surely want others to be blessed, it is vital to focus on receiving God's blessings for yourself as well. This is stressed because many people are hesitant to accept more good for themselves. Such reluctance may stem from old beliefs of not deserving more or limited concepts of what they need or want.

You certainly do not want your good to pass you by, so affirm and accept that you deserve ALL of the rich good that God has for you. Believe that you are ready to accept it now.

Believe that what you declare is true. There is no room for doubt; you either believe or you do not. Have faith in what you declare and accept that it is Truth. Then give thanks, and be sincerely grateful. Imagine your gratitude if you had just been handed the keys to a brand new luxury car and told that it was is yours.

All channels of financial supply are open to me now and I am richly, bountifully, and beautifully prospered in every good way.

It is not beneficial to declare the Prayer-Treatment affirmations and then wonder if it will happen, or to insist that it will come only through familiar channels--if it comes at all! As stated before, some people erroneously mentally limit the number of channels through which their good may come.

Upon being given the Prayer-Treatment for "unexpected" income, one person read it through and began to affirm it. However, he immediately decided that the only possible way for more money to come was through his job. It took some doing to convince him to open his thinking to other possibilities, but he eventually did. A short time later, a friend, whom he had done a favor for, months earlier, showed up and insisted on giving him $100.00.

Now he was convinced! This was proof that there truly are more channels through which he can receive financial income. He went on to demonstrate more "unexpected" income, including an all-expense-paid trip to Hawaii for his wife and himself.

There is significance in placing no limits on the channels through which your financial supply may come. It is also empowering to think of yourself as being prospered *richly, bountifully,* and *beautifully.*

The Universe has unfathomable riches just waiting to be claimed. Although sometimes people do, it is unthinkable to entertain the idea of smallness when it comes to God's supply. His supply is abundant and beautiful.

How do *you* want to be prospered? Will you be satisfied with just a small increase, only mediocre amounts? Would you prefer, on the other hand, to be prospered in large amounts? Believe that you deserve nothing less than the abundance of the richest blessings that the Universe can offer.

When you begin receiving more of the rich good the Universe has for you, your prosperity will also be beautiful! As you accept only the best, you will be prospered in *every* good way. Accept only the best! To be *beautifully* prospered is far more exciting than some kind of dull, limited prosperity!

A woman had spent many years in limiting her financial life. Upon being given a copy of the Prayer-Treatment for "unexpected" income, she became excited when she read about being *richly, bountifully and beautifully prospered.*

Part of her excitement was because it sounded so much better than a life of dull, uninteresting existence. Moreover she realized that she had limited her good by viewing the Universe as penurious, and refusing to accept what is hers by divine right.

She began a daily declaration of all of the statements in the Prayer-Treatment, but especially focused on the statement: *All channels of financial supply are open to me now, and I am richly, bountifully, and beautifully prospered in every good way.*

She now understood the need to impress upon her mind this new idea and to mentally surround herself with the kind of riches she really wanted. She wanted to be done with the old lack-producing belief system and to accept a new, rich, beautiful, and bountiful life-style.

At first her demonstrations were rather small and infrequent, but as she persisted, they happened more often and became larger. She was excited and approached each new day with an air of expectancy. She said, "While I am expecting to be richly, bountifully, and beautifully prospered, it happens in the most amazing and unusual ways! For instance, just today, I received a check from someone who had owed me money for several years. Thinking I would never receive it, I had forgotten about it long ago."

She added, "Then a friend gave me a lead to a sale from which I received a handsome commission. I cannot possibly list all the small and large financial blessings that have come to me since I began to daily affirm the Prayer-Treatment for 'unexpected' income. In taking stock of my life now, I know that I am richly, bountifully, and beautifully prospered in every good way! I am truly grateful."

She eventually demonstrated a loving, generous and wealthy husband , who sees to it that she lives richly, bountifully and beautifully!

8

"Right" Demonstrations

I believe true prosperity includes the demonstration of right living conditions, right activity and genuine happiness.

Unfortunately, some people believe that their lot in life is to struggle, eke out a living, and live a drab, colorless life. To them, prosperity is something that, if it comes at all, won't amount to much. How sad for them! They could just as easily enjoy a life of plenty, live bountifully and beautifully, and have a lot of fun doing so.

What do you believe about prosperity? Have you put limitations on it? Have you been too willing to settle for less and live in surroundings you don't really enjoy? On the contrary, is your life filled with the kind of activity that keeps life interesting and worth living? Are you as happy and fulfilled as you want to be?

These questions are asked to challenge your thinking, to encourage you to take a good look at your belief systems and your acceptance level.

If you do not fully believe and accept that the Universe wants you to live splendidly, and demonstrate in accord with that, you can *change your thinking!* True prosperity absolutely includes the demonstration of right living conditions, right activity and genuine happiness.

Right living conditions means to be beautifully clothed, housed and transported in the manner that makes you feel best. You can demonstrate these circumstances through the use of your own mind power according to the spiritual laws and principles that govern true prosperity. Demonstration is the manifestion of your desired good in your life.

You don't have to live extravagantly in a palatial mansion with servants to be prosperous. There's nothing wrong with that, but the idea is to live without want, to easily have what you desire to live beautifully and happily. Your surroundings are up to you; it is your prerogative to make them just as pleasant as possible. The "place" where you really live is in your mind and you should make that as beautiful as you can!

Right activity is wholesome and positive, and never harms anyone. It benefits all who may be affected in any way by what you do. Through right activity, you can empower others to benefit, directly and indirectly, by your actions.

There is never a need to engage in dishonest or unscrupulous ventures in order to gain riches. That kind of behavior may seem to bring prosperity for a time, but the eventual price is far higher than anyone would want to pay. The cost is high and value low because such activity is not founded in love.

Genuine happiness comes through getting in touch with the real energy of right living conditions and activity. That energy is love and empowers you to live life lovingly, happily and prosperously.

By putting lots of love into all you do, you build a solid foundation under your activity which results in true happiness--the kind that wells up from deep within and spills over into the lives of others. Loved ones, friends, co-workers and business associates will benefit along with you. That is the essence of true prosperity and brings joy in accomplishment.

A man awakened one day to discover that what he had was not very exciting or satisfying. He had struggled, sometimes in questionable ways, to make a living. He had few friends, and felt that he could do without those. He wisely made a decision to change his ways, not an easy thing to do, but he was determined. He sought out teachers and books from which to learn and was surprised at how things began to change!

He learned a new way of thinking, accepting God as the Source of his supply, using prosperity affirmations, and through this process, began to like himself. Liking himself was surprisingly easy because he had formerly thought of himself with disgust. His prosperity grew in wonderful ways and he thought he couldn't be happier. However joy kept coming up from deep within--direct from the ever-flowing fountain of God's infinite and omnipresent love.

This word which I speak in faith believing activates the law of INCREASED universal good for me , and I EXPECT to see rich results now!

The "word" referred to is the whole of the Prayer-Treatment. It appears as many words, but in this case encompasses the word of Truth. It is the declaration of Truth.

Charles Fillmore, the co-founder of Unity, wrote in *Prosperity, "The secret to demonstration is to conceive what is true in Being and to carry out the concept in thought, word, and act."*

As you declare all of the words of the Prayer-Treatment, you are affirming that they are true; that you believe it to be so. Your affirming does not *make* them true, but is the realization that they are *already* true. Further, you are accepting that your declarations activate universal substance, which will manifest in the form of expected and unexpected financial blessings.

A reader in Missouri wrote: "When I first received the Prayer-Treatment for 'unexpected' income, and read it through, it sounded good because it seemed to be in accord with what I already believed. However, I had not actually vocalized the words. Following the instructions, I began declaring the Prayer-Treatment affirmations daily.

"After about four days, I received a refund check for $70.68, then received a $160.00 refund from my mother's hospitalization. I was invited to attend a $100.00 workshop, free. To my amazement, I received a check for $140.00 from a utility company.

"Also, I have a lot more energy and seem to accomplish more than usual. It is wonderful to wake up in the morning, affirm the Prayer-Treatment and have the great feeling that some good things will happen today!"

Yes, good things do happen when you use the Prayer-Treatment, and expect them to.

A person in Minnesota reported: "I began using the Prayer-Treatment for 'unexpected' income immediately after receiving it. I followed the instructions for about a week, and one day I received $450.00 for a typing job done for a friend. I didn't expect to be paid, but was thrilled that it happened.

"The Prayer-Treatment and my demonstration have helped to change my attitude and outlook. It is true, as you wrote to me, that more is on its way to me now. I have just received two additional sums of money and some gifts. 'Unexpected' income is a wonderful idea; the best part is--it works!"

9

Claim and Accept

I visualize the financial good I expect. I see it coming to me now, richly and abundantly.

Visualization is an important part of using the Prayer-Treatment for "unexpected" income because it involves the exercise of your wonderful imagination.

It is essential for you to spend some time in mentally picturing the financial increase you are expecting as well as demonstrating high-powered faith. In fact using your imagination gives more power to your faith.

In your imagination, you can give form to your desired increase. Attempt to "see" with your mind, the desired good, then pour the substance of your faith into that mold. When you do so, a mega-force is established that literally draws to you the expected good, even though it may come in *unexpected* ways.

Some people have a vague concept of the increased prosperity that they desire. It may be due to fear, because they are accustomed to thinking in limited ways; or a long held belief that one must work hard for every dollar. Sometimes people suffer from mental laziness, and don't consciously use their imaginations to create increased financial supply. If they could only recognize how powerful the imagination can be, they would devote more time and attention to using it positively and productively.

Your imagination is powerful, and it is wise to spend time in visualizing what you want. If you have difficulty visualizing, practice by focusing on visual objects, closing your eyes and trying to "see" them with your imagination. If you still cannot visualize, then try to form word pictures in your mind. The important thing is to hold in mind, the best you can, that which you want to have or achieve.

There is a law of mind and manifestation that goes like this: **M I E, M**ind **I**dea **E**xpression.

First is mind the idea, then expression of the idea, much as a sculptor sees the statue in the stone, or a painter sees the finished piece before beginning to paint. Imagination and faith work together in putting on canvas, what the painter sees with his mind while letting fingers and brush do the work. So it is with helping to bring forth the increased income you desire.

Take some time now, close your eyes, and allow yourself to "see" in your imagination, the financial good you desire. Create a vivid picture of cash; see people giving you money--often! Hold the picture clearly in mind and see yourself gratefully receiving. Let it be real, in living color, so that you may have the feeling that it is already yours, because it is! Accept in faith, give thanks, and move on.

Remember to see your good coming to you *richly and abundantly.* There is no room for mediocrity. *The Universe never limits its provision or the quality of that provision, and neither should you.* It is just as easy to visualize plenty of the best as a little of poor quality. The subconscious mind does not know the difference; it will give you what you envision, and believe to be true.

When a person having difficulty in demonstrating "unexpected" income, asked for help, she said that she was faithfully affirming the Prayer-Treatment every day. However, when asked if she was visualizing the financial increase, she said, no, she didn't think that it was of great importance, and it didn't come naturally for her.

It was suggested that she spend some time visualizing the desired good, and it was explained to her why the using of the imagination is essential to demonstrating greater financial supply. She agreed to try because she very much wanted to increase her prosperity, to know firsthand if this technique actually worked.

About a week later, she reported that after spending a few minutes daily visualizing what she wants while using the Prayer-Treatment, she received an "unexpected' IRS refund check in the mail. (Now, THAT *is unexpected!*)

She had actually expected to owe more money, but apparently, an error had been made. Her refund was for $358.00--what a wonderful surprise!

She has received other amounts also, and is getting that wonderful feeling that comes from using the Prayer-Treatment, visualizing, and receiving "unexpected" income. Now, she is a firm believer!

As you declare the words of the Prayer-Treatment each day, take a few moments and visualize money. Determine how much more you desire, perhaps for a new car, home, travel, or other good purposes. How much would those things cost? "See" that money coming to you easily, better yet, *see yourself with the money now.*

If you desire a new car, picture yourself owning and driving it. Use the Prayer-Treatment, then let the money come in God's own good way. It will or you may demonstrate that new car in another way.

Visualize other things that you want and see yourself having them now. Often people tend to imagine negative things coming or happening to them. They pour worry into those molds and wonder why negative things happen, or question why the good they desire is delayed. Nothing positive is accomplished by worry. Keep it positive.

Not only is it important to monitor your thinking and the words you speak, but also to watch what you are picturing in your mind. There is supreme power in using your imagination to "see" the financial good you expect coming to you NOW, richly and abundantly!

I claim and accept it for myself now.

Make your claim on the Universe for what you expect to receive; you deserve it just as much as anyone. Of course, while claiming your good, you do not in any way take away from others.

Imagine sitting at a banquet table piled high with all kinds of beautiful, tasty food. Not much will happen unless you dig in. You can sit and admire it and go away hungry. Some people do by *failing to claim what is rightfully theirs.* When you are invited to the banquet table, help yourself!

You have been invited, as an honored guest, to Life's banquet table of rich abundance. It is provided for you by a loving, all-giving Father Who wants you to help yourself. Daily affirming the Prayer-Treatment empowers you to *stake your claim.* Use the tools you have been given by a loving Universe.

Not only is it essential for you to stake your claim but to accept it also. At Life's banquet table, you may claim and accept what is yours by putting whatever you want on your plate. (Bring a BIG plate!) More than enough is yours so claim and accept it NOW!

A reader in New York wrote: "I am writing this letter with a thankful heart. Since using the Prayer-Treatment for 'unexpected' income, I received just over $1000.00 in extra income as part of a bonus plan. I did not expect to receive that much so you will understand my excitement. I must tell you that it didn't happen until I really opened my mind to plenty and decided to definitely claim and accept much more than I had.

"I am now expecting more money so that I can finish paying off bills. I am looking forward with faith believing and seeing much more coming to me now. Praise God. It works!"

An "unexpected" income fan in Utah wrote: "Today I unexpectedly received $474.50 in the mail, and received a $50.00 refund on an exercise class. My husband received an unexpected bonus of $80.00 in his paycheck. We also received $75.00 from selling an old tape recorder,

$20.00 for some tires and there was $14.00 extra in my paycheck! God is good and we thank Him. We are now getting caught up financially. I almost forgot--I also won $200.00 in merchandise this week! It works!"

I am grateful in advance! I bless all the good I have now, and I bless the increase.

An attitude of gratitude is essential. It is through a grateful heart that your good comes more rapidly. The friendly Universe loves to pour forth Its rich good, especially for those who receive cheerfully and express gratitude both silently and audibly.

The "Gratitude Attitude" is covered more completely in Chapter Thirteen, but following are some ideas for starters.

It is essential to be grateful *in advance,* although it is easier to be grateful *after* receiving. It may be difficult for some people to be thankful *before* receiving, especially those who have had very little and have struggled to get enough to live on. However, lack of gratitude is often the cause of financial struggle. Do not under estimate the value of being grateful in advance.

A good example was given by Jesus Christ, the Master Prosperity Teacher, when He spoke His word, Lazarus, who had been dead for days, emerged from the cave alive! Jesus gave thanks beforehand that His prayer had been heard and answered.

You may be sure that Jesus used his imagination to "see" Lazarus alive. When performing His miracles, He always gave thanks in advance. By expressing thanks BEFOREHAND, He put the finishing touch on His declaration of faith, and His prayer was answered immediately.

You have the same dynamic power. By giving thanks *before* your expected good arrives regardless of appearances, you send out a positive magnetic force which will literally attract your desired outcome.

Give thanks in advance even though you do not know how your good is coming. You don't need to know how--be grateful that it is. Give thanks before receiving, in faith that the Universe is cooperating with you. This creates EXPECTANCY. *Expect to receive and you will.*

Blessing is high-powered activity and cursing is negative energy. Don't curse negative experiences unless you want them to stay with you. It is far better to bless them and to look for the good. As you do, negative experiences will lessen and positive situations will increase. Blessing is prospering energy and will bring more peace of mind.

A sure way of increasing your good is to bless what you already have. Look around and see what you have, and if you have not blessed it lately, now is a good time to do so. Perhaps there is someone or something that you may have neglected while blessing other things. Bless them now and do it often! Every day I bless my family, friends, home and everything in it, car, finances, and I especially bless my readers! God bless *you!*

Take your wallet and checkbook in your hands and bless them. Note how much money you have on hand and in the bank. Bless that money and give thanks for it. Especially bless your outstanding bills with the rich substance of the Universe that is now coming to pay them. Bless all the channels through which your increased prosperity is coming to you.

Now picture in your mind your desired financial increase, and give thanks, and bless it as though it had already appeared. Allow yourself to get the *feeling* of having it now. As you do, you empower yourself to attract happy financial surprises--wonderful gifts of money and many other good things. Finally, bless yourself for the wonderful person you are.

A young businessman began declaring the Prayer-Treatment for "unexpected" income when he desperately needed more money, and wanted his business to prosper. He was unfamiliar with the practice of blessing things, believing that was the work of priests, ministers and other religious leaders. However, after becoming convinced that he had the same power and authority, he decided to try the blessing technique.

He immediately stopped condemning himself and his business for not prospering. Instead, he blessed everything--his clients (silently while in their presence), and every other aspect of his business. To his delight, things quickly began to improve, and as he continued to bless and daily affirm the Prayer-Treatment, new clients appeared and his business flourished. His grateful blessing attitude was paying off handsomely!

What do you desire? Get it clearly in mind, give thanks in advance, and be sincerely grateful. Blessing all of the good you now have as well as blessing the increase that you are expecting, will hasten the appearance of your good. It seems to know exactly where you are because of the positive signal being sent out. That signal is love and love attracts its own.

Gratitude and blessing are love in expression. The more you bless and give thanks, the more love is expressed, making of yourself an irresistible magnet for universal good which loves to move into *your* life!

A businessman in Illinois wrote: "Today I received $150.00 in the mail toward a long-forgotten debt. Talk about *unexpected income!* I was amazed since I had declared the Prayer-Treatment affirmations for only a week. I am grateful!"

A woman in New Jersey reported: "For a time there was some doubt as to my continuing to receive a small income for work I was doing, To my surprise, not only is it continuing, but I was given a $25.00 increase. Thanks for the 'unexpected' income idea."

10

Share the Good

I bless all others who are using this Prayer-Treatment for "unexpected" income. I KNOW we are ALL prospering together in every good way, and we share the good we receive.

Blessing people is the same as blessing things. There is no way of knowing how many people are using the Prayer-Treatment for "unexpected" income each day. However, you may be assured that they number in the thousands, and increase daily. Think for a moment about that kind of power! Ten thousand people multiply the power of what you do--at least ten thousand times!

As you send out your blessing to everyone using the Prayer-Treatment, they are doing the same for you, multiplying the activity that gathers increasing energy. The energy is love, therefore blessing others is giving love to them and spreads love all over our planet. There is no other activity as powerful for good as this!

Love is the great mega-force of the universe and the fulfilling energy that works miracles .

Blessing everyone is a demonstration of unselfishness. It is also an expanding activity of the mind and helps more than you may realize to avoid placing limitations on the good that can come to you. You will be affirming that you are willing for everyone to experience the same blessings that you desire. Your desire is for increased financial income, expanding growth, happiness and fulfillment for all--that's good thinking!

Now, think of the thousands of people wanting the same for you. The fact that you may not know each other doesn't matter. By blessing them, and they you, all participate in a very powerful, loving and prospering activity. Accept that you are on the receiving end--that you are an irresistible magnet for increased good, and everyone is rooting for and supporting you.

You cannot, by accepting your good, keep good from anyone else. There is more than enough for everyone! Accept, in faith, that ALL are now prospering together and in every good way. Do not think for a moment, that by taking your fair share, you can deplete the Source or take away from anyone. You cannot! By claiming and accepting what is yours by divine right, you are helping to circulate substance and the Universe wants you to do that!

As you bless everyone else, and know that they too are prospering, you will help them to accept their rich good and move even more of that good into manifestation. It's a wonderful cooperative activity in which everyone is helping to prosper our planet and all its people.

As you receive your "unexpected" income, share it freely. First, give your tithe--10% of all you receive, back to God, the Source. Then pay bills, buy a gift for someone, take friends or loved ones to dinner or a movie, buy something you need--or don't need but only desire. That's good for the economy and spreads the riches around for the benefit of others too.

An *"unexpected" income believer in Wyoming wrote:* "Thank you for such a practical way to use my mind to bring more prosperity into my life. I am convinced it works. I was looking for a job, and not only found a good one, the salary is more than I had hoped for.

"One of the things that impressed me was that so many other people are doing the same thing, which created a great positive prayer power. It was empowering for me to accept that *their* power, even though they do not know me, is aimed at me. It helps to know that I was doing something good for others too.

"Blessing is obviously a powerful 'tool' to use for creating more prosperity for myself as well as for others. I have learned that it pays to put God first, financially, and to expect *'unexpected'* income."

From California: "It has been a month since I received the information about 'unexpected' Income and the Prayer-Treatment. I began using it right away but I waited until now to contact you because I wanted to use it on my own. Doing exactly as instructed, I read aloud the Prayer-Treatment twice each day. The results were astonishing! I received $267.00 in 'unexpected' Income!

"I work as the manager of an apartment complex and receive free rent, but I receive only a small salary. The 'unexpected' income was most welcome! Other good things are happening too and I am much happier and feel healthier. My whole family seems to be positively affected because of this prospering activity.

"It is wonderful to know that so many others are praying this Prayer-Treatment with me and blessing me, as I am surely blessing everyone! This is a great activity and I am *expecting* more 'unexpected' income."

As you affirm the Prayer-Treatment for "unexpected" income, know that your blessing will come back to you richly and abundantly. Everyone else is enjoying the same rich good. In sharing the good that you receive, countless other people are richly blessed, too.

Blessing others is a positive activity that helps make the whole world better and indirectly benefits those who may know nothing of what is being done. It positively adds to and builds up world consciousness.

I now freely give my tenth to God's good work. My giving makes me rich.

The giving of the tithe, your tenth, back to God is an ancient practice that is just as effective today as it was in biblical times. While this subject is covered more thoroughly in Chapter Twelve, it is introduced here because it has a definite connection to your success in demonstrating "unexpected" income.

Tithing is a conscious recognition of God as the Source of all supply. It will dynamically empower you to prosper as no other universal prosperity law.

Catherine Ponder, writing in, *The Millionaire Moses,* said, "Since ancient times it has been proved that those who tithe ten percent of their income to God's work find that their prosperity increases by leaps and bounds, until all fear of poverty has disappeared. The act of tithing gives your prosperity a permanent, enduring basis. *To practice tithing is a fascinating and mystical way to be prospered.*"

She has certainly proved the prosperity law of tithing in her financial life. Through her books and lectures, and from other teachers, I learned to tithe and would not be without it today.

When I made the decision many years ago to prove the tithing law for myself, it was perhaps the best decision I have ever made. I thank Catherine Ponder for helping to convince me to tithe and give her credit for this. She has convinced many others to tithe as well, and as a result to prosper. You, too, will prosper by reading her many prosperity books, and by tithing.

If you are serious about having "unexpected" financial and other riches bless your life, it is essential to accept that tithing is a necessary action on your part. While it is powerful to speak the words of the Prayer-Treatment, tithing adds a dimension that will bring about practical action and mystically prosper you. This will not happen for those who use the Prayer-Treatment faithfully but leave out the giving of their tenth to God.

It is insufficient for you to speak the words and then neglect to "put your money where your mouth is," as the saying goes.

When you receive "unexpected" income, it is important to give ten percent of that amount to God's work. If it is a small sum, you may want to set it aside and add to it before you give. However, make sure you do give your tithe because it will complete the circle.

A woman in Illinois wrote: "I had sold candy to raise money for a young lady in a contest. One couple had not paid me and I had mentally written it off as a loss. When encountering the man in a restaurant one day, he said, 'I owe you $12.00 don't I?' I didn't have my record book with me but accepted the $12.00 which was both needed and unexpected. Here is my tithe.

"I should have known that God would somehow see to it that I was compensated because of my being a tither. I am so grateful that you convinced me to tithe. Since beginning to do so, my prosperity has increased. When first using the Prayer-Treatment for 'unexpected' income, I thought I could just skip the part about tithing, because I didn't understand the need to give back to the Source.

"When I began to include tithing, small 'unexpected' prospering things started to happen. The one I have reported is just one of many. I would not stop the practice of tithing now. I am convinced that it is my ticket to the much larger prosperity that I want."

Your giving does make you rich; giving is the first part of receiving.

When I was a boy growing up on the
Oregon coast in the thirties, we had a well with
a hand pump. We had to prime the pump with
water in order to get the water to come up out
of the well. The water simply would not cooperate
until we primed the pump. In other words, we
had to give what we wanted to receive. An
interesting thing happened when the pump was
primed with a little water. *We got a lot more
water in return!* That is the way it is with tithing
--when giving back to the Source ten percent of
all you receive, it will be multiplied many times
and returned to you!

Through my many years in the ministry, I
have discovered that some people try hard to
prosper but do not understand the principle of
giving before getting. They focus their energy
upon improving their financial status while
ignoring the most important part--giving
generously first. If you want the Universe to give
freely to you, it is essential for you to give in the
same way.

Along with giving it is good to declare often:
MY GIVING MAKES ME RICH! Declare it over
and over until you are convinced that it is true.
As you do, you will cause universal substance to
cooperate and move toward you. It will free you
to receive and enjoy more of the wonderful rich
good that is your destiny.

*Whatever you
ask in prayer,
believe that you
receive it,
and you will.*

– Mark 11:24

11

Declare Your Faith

God gives to me rich, lavish, happy financial blessings now!

This declaration puts a crowning touch on the rest of the Prayer-Treatment. You are consciously accepting that what you declare is true and it is bearing good fruit now. You are acknowledging that God does nothing mediocre or inferior, but will send *rich* and *lavish* financial blessings. The best.

When you use the Prayer-Treatment, You have *every* right to *expect* the "windows of heaven" to open and pour the richest of blessings into your life. It is also your divine right, as the child of a rich Father, to *accept* the beautiful and bountiful supply that your heavenly Father wants you to have.

Further, in making this declaration you are acknowledging that God is the source of *all* supply and in particular *your* supply. He *is* giving his best financial blessings to you *now*, and you don't have to wait. Since *now* is the only time there is, it is right that you accept your rich good *now*. You may choose to procrastinate until some time in the future, but why do that when it is easy and more fun to accept it *now*. As the saying goes, "there is no time like the present" for you to enjoy "unexpected" income!

From New York "Things are coming along just fine now that I have accepted that God wants to give me much richer financial blessings than I have accepted before. That was when I thought I was not good enough to have anything better, but that has all changed.

"I have paid off all my bills ahead of time this month. There have also been new, positive developments. I am in the process of locating my perfect job where I can serve God best. Last week I received a telephone call from a very successful businessman who is president of his own company. He is very knowledgeable and influential, and has given me extremely helpful guidance. He has also introduced me to some positive people.

"He gave me a set of important books worth over $500.00. It is simply amazing how things are coming together for me now. The Prayer-Treatment for 'unexpected' income is making a positive difference, has helped to change my attitude, and is already increasing my prosperity. I'm excited about what is happening and what I know is on the way to me. I am so thankful!"

Accept the rich, lavish financial and all the other wonderful gifts God has for you. Allow yourself to open up and receive because God does not limit His supply and neither should you. He will never stint on quality either, so accept plenty of the best and do it now!

This is so now. I am grateful. Thank You, Father!

Declaring, "This is so now" puts a finishing touch on the entire Prayer-Treatment. By recognizing and accepting that what you have declared is so, you know beyond a doubt that "unexpected" income *is coming* to you. You believe, not that it *may* come, or *if God deems you fit,* He will give you *some* unexpected income, or *hope* that you will receive happy, financial "surprises.", you KNOW it is true RIGHT NOW!

You especially make this declaration in the calm assurance that using the Prayer-Treatment is effective and your mental activity will bring desired results. There is no guessing, on the contrary, you confidently accept that by declaring the Prayer-Treatment faithfully you will improve your financial condition. It will improve through the receiving of "unexpected" income PLUS what you are already receiving.

In effect you are helping to open the prosperity floodgates and allow good things to come to you. This activity is different than what you have done before because it is altogether prosperity-producing.

Since you have made your declarations in faith believing, you may now look for those happy financial "surprises." They know where you are and are making their way to you; know and accept this NOW.

NOW is the only time there is, Therefore what you have declared is true NOW. Again, you do not have to *wait* for it or hope it is real, but only know that it is. Consequently, it is important that you ACT AS THOUGH IT IS ALREADY SO, because it is, and you may as well accept it in faith.

That should be reason enough for being grateful and declaring it. Let your heart be deeply thankful exactly as if your most cherished desire had been fulfilled. Think how you will feel and then declare your gratitude to the Source of your good--the loving, all-providing Father-God.

Your heavenly Father does not really need to be thanked, but in some mystical way, by directing your *thanks* toward the Source, you make a better connection with It. Your acknowledgment helps to cause universal riches to flow more freely into your life, and gives a glorious climax to the Prayer-Treatment. Let your gratitude be full and joyfully expressed in the words. *"Thank You, Father!"*

Accepting the truth now brings rich dividends: "When I received the Prayer-Treatment for "unexpected" income, I began to use it immediately because my need was urgent. It gave me strong motivation to try something new and accept in faith that it is true. I put all the faith I could into what I was doing. Within a week I received $15.00 for a forgotten item that another person had sold for me knowing that would be acceptable.

"That $15.00 may not seem like a lot, but it sure came in handy--much more so than the old item that was doing me no good.

"More money came to me, in smaller amounts except for an unexpected check from a grateful friend for whom I had done a favor--that check was for $150.00. I felt like a millionaire! Thanks for this great idea. It is sure working good for me and I am grateful." - - *From New Mexico.*

Gratitude results in "unexpected" income: "Here is my 'unexpected' income report. Last month I received a total of 100.00 and the previous month, a total of $205.00. The $100.00 had been owed to me for some time and I had all but given up on ever getting it, but that was before I began giving thanks--and being genuinely grateful--for everything. I am especially grateful for the 'unexpected' income that I know is coming to me.

"I wanted to send my tithe and make my report as soon as possible to keep it flowing and because I am so grateful to God. I am sure my gratitude is causing much more to come to me. I have started a new job as a legal secretary and, for the first time, have my own office which I can decorate as I wish. I am sure that using the Prayer-Treatment and my grateful attitude have a lot to do with all the blessings that I am now receiving. Believe me--I am grateful!"
- - *From Indiana*

How to Have "Unexpected" Income

A short report from California: "I received $120.00 cash in the mail that I wasn't expecting, I am so grateful!"

Receives unexpected blessings: "Thank you for your prayers with mine for 'unexpected' income. I have been able to take advantage of special prices on home furnishings, tires, clothing, and hotel accommodations. I have also received extra cash and a bonus. I love it! The Gratitude Attitude helps as well." - *From Arizona*

From Louisiana: I have just received a raise of $180.00, and have been asked out to dinner so frequently, my grocery bill is down. I have traveled out of town so my utilities bill is down, too. I am looking forward with great anticipation to more. I like 'unexpected' income! Needless to say, I am grateful. I thank God, my Source, daily for all the expected and 'unexpected' good coming to me."

Bring all the tithes—
the whole tenth of your income—
into the storehouse,
that there may be food in
My house, and prove
Me now by it, says the Lord
of hosts, if I will not open
the windows of heaven for you
and pour you out a blessing,
that there shall not be room
enough to receive it.

-- Malachi 3:10
(Amplified Old Testament)

12

Why Tithe?

A person who began tithing a few years ago soon saw his income start to grow. He no longer worried about money and he did not experience financial strain or undesirable surprises. Instead, since starting to tithe, his financial surprises were good ones.

Tithing and using the Prayer-Treatment for "unexpected" income, caused money to come to him "out of the blue." In addition, he was surprised at how much further his money went. He said that tithing seems to have a rubberizing effect in that it somehow causes money to stretch.

Giving a tenth of your whole income to God's good work helps to bring rich financial increase and protect you from negative experiences. Tithing makes a "divine connection"* with the Source of all wealth. It is one of the surest ways I know to verify within your consciousness that God is the Source of your supply, and establish a link with the supply itself.

Another good thing about tithing is that it helps to eliminate those negative "financial surprises" that no one needs. Those surprises sometimes come in the form of car repairs, doctor bills and other things requiring money that you would rather use for something more enjoyable.

The more you consciously and financially connect with the Source, the easier life will become, with less worry about financial matters. Because you know where your supply is--within yourself and everywhere present--you won't have to look very far. It is always where you are!

*See "Divine Connection" in the author's book, *Power Words for Prosperous Living!*

Tithing helps to open your mind to rich ideas. Many people have been exceedingly prospered through tithing. For example, LeTourneau was given the idea of the huge earth-moving machines from which he became a multi-millionaire. Many exceptionally wealthy people attribute their financial success to tithing.

What is a tithe?

A tithe is ten percent of your whole income, *before* deductions, not 1% or 5% but 10%. Some metaphysical teachers may tell you that it is okay to start out with 1% or 5% and build up to 10%. However, if you are serious about prosperity and have a desire for the law of increase to work fully for you, boldly give your full ten percent at the beginning and continue to do so. *Make a decision to change your financial status and boldly carry out that plan.*

If you want the Universe to give full measure you must give in the same way. You cannot afford to fool around with less than the full 10%. You do not want only a portion of the riches that the Source has for you, but the "whole enchilada" as the saying goes. Do your part and God will never fail to do His.

I know through experience how difficult it can be to start giving 10% back to God. I struggled with it for quite a while until I realized that I had to do something. I made a bold decision to give the full 10%, and put the tithing law to the test It worked! If you truly want to take a positive step toward eliminating financial lack, then take the plunge, start with 10%, and keep it up. You will take a big step toward financial abundance.

A tithe is not a gift nor is it charity. Neither is it a reward or payment for services. Do not use your tithe to pay bills or to help relatives and friends. When you want to help others financially, give them "seed money" and claim your tenfold return on that. Make sure that you use your tithe for nothing but to further God's good work.

In other words, give back to God, 10% and use the rest for other things. Take it off the top and give it *first* before using the money for anything else. When you make a habit of giving to God first, you'll be surprised at how far your money goes.

If you think you cannot afford to tithe and must use the money for personal things, you do not yet understand the Law of Increase. Seek more understanding until it becomes clear that giving a full ten percent back to the Source is the surest and most practical way for you to establish continual financial plenty for yourself. Remember that the tithe is God's money which you have no right to use for anything except to further His work.

Do not wait until you fully understand the Law of Increase. Put your faith into what you do and trust the Universe to respond to the faith you have placed in It. It may surprise you--especially when you give in love and joy.

Where should you give your tithe?

Give your tithe to a church or spiritual organization, minister or other person who is directly involved in God's work. It is best to give where you are receiving your spiritual food. Do not continue to give financially to any organization with which you are no longer involved. Support those who are feeding you spiritually, especially those from whom you learn the dynamic laws, principles and activity that will increase your prosperity. In so doing, you place yourself in direct relation to the Source.

Would you like to have a rich relative Who can really support you? God is the richest relative you could ever have! His resources are limitless and are yours for the asking, appropriating and receiving when you act in harmony with His laws and principles.

Where you give your tithe is of utmost importance. While it is okay to spread your tithe around, it is best to make your tithe checks as large as possible which will help to bring larger increase to you.

What are the results of tithing?

One of the unexpected benefits of tithing is that it will give you divine protection, shielding you from many of the negative aspects of life. It gives you greater wisdom to use your money more intelligently. When I have found it necessary to really look to God for increase, I knew, because of being a long-standing tither, that everything would be taken care of. I am divinely protected so there is nothing to fear. Thus I relax, let go, and let God take care of things which He *always* does.

You can expect to receive ten, twenty, fifty and even a hundredfold increase. Do not ask me how that is; it just is! One of the reasons may be that, by tithing, you establish a divine partnership with the Source in which God is the senior Partner, and His resources are infinite. This activity seems to have an accumulative and multiplying effect.

You simply cannot out-give God! Try your best, it cannot be done, and you couldn't ask for a better "financial connection." God never fails; He never has and never will! If you are not already doing so, the most advantageous thing you can do is to begin and continue to tithe.

A businesswoman made an agreement with God when she opened a new store. She agreed to give back to God 10% of all she received, right off the top. From the beginning, her new business prospered--far greater than she had thought possible.

A Chiropractor and his wife, starting out quite a number of years ago, learned of the value of tithing and made a covenant to give at least 10% of their earnings back to God. They did so faithfully although at first they struggled to get their practice going.

Sometimes, one or the other would call and ask for prayers to help them meet a financial need. At those times, I would remind them that since they were tithers, there was nothing to worry about; God would provide. He always did and continues to so--abundantly!

Today, they have a thriving practice where they are helping large numbers of people to be healthier and feel better. They live in a lovely, spacious home in a beautiful neighborhood and drive luxury automobiles.

From Illinois: "About a week after using the affirmation, TITHING FROM MY WHOLE INCOME, I AM NOW PROSPERED, AND MY LIFE IS HAPPY AND COMPLETE, my husband and I got to go on a vacation to California. We stayed three weeks with little expense and had a delightful time.

"We were both unemployed and hadn't tithed for about two months when we decided to start again. I sent in my tithe and continued to affirm that God is truly the Source of our supply and will provide His own amazing channels for our prosperity.

"The day I sent the tithe my husband heard of a good paying job, and two days later he got it. I have gone on an interview and will also be starting back to work soon. Thanks for helping us realize the importance of giving our tenth back to God. We have learned our lesson and will continue tithing. It works!"

Another important result of tithing is better health, which is a natural result of being freed from worrying due to the lack of money. Money worries are one of the leading causes of ill health. They can cause fear, frustration and resentment. When you tithe, you are empowered with a kind of freedom and peace of mind which seem to come in no other way.

Still another effect of tithing is the joy and happiness that come through having an intimate relationship with the Source. It enables you to relax and go about your daily activity confidently, knowing that everything is provided for. Whatever you may need, God will provide.

Receives Christmas bonus! "Sometimes in our busy schedules and trying to make ends meet, we forget about the opportunity to increase our abundance. This was my case recently when I realized that it had been a while since I had tithed.

"When I was given the opportunity at two Christmas candelighting services, without hesitation I did, and it felt so good! A few days later, I received an unexpected Christmas bonus from one of my employers. Here is my grateful tithe from this 'unexpected' income."
                              -- A reader in California.

From Oregon: "I am happy to report that since beginning to tithe, my health as well as my wealth have had a *healing* experience. They are both doing a lot better!"

Receives pay increase: "Not only was I able to take a really super vacation, I've been offered a new job that pays over $4,000.00 per year more than the one I had lost. I am so thankful that I kept on tithing and using the Prayer-Treatment for 'unexpected' income. Together they have worked miracles in my life! I have a new attitude of positive expectancy. I am grateful"
                              - - From Ohio

From California: "On the last Sunday in December, I had the pleasure of giving my first Sunday morning lesson at the Religious Science church where I've attended for several years. My talk was basically about prosperity and tithing in particular. I used an article from your newsletter about the businessman who rediscovered the need to tithe. The talk was well received, probably because I spoke with authority from my experience as a tither for many years."

Tithing brings cash: "For some reason, my tithing brings greater prosperity in the form of cash. I consider myself to be prosperous in some areas, but I now allow cash to be an even larger part of my experience. I accept it with gratitude in whatever form it comes!"   - - *From California*

Those who are truly prosperous know the value of "ten" in relation to prosperity. "Ten" is the magic number of increase used successfully by prosperous people of ancient times as well as in modern times. People who prosper accept without question the value of voluntarily tithing ten percent of their whole income to God's work where they are learning the prospering truth.

Does tithing really work?

Yes, it has always worked for those who practice it faithfully in the right attitude. To be most effective, tithing should be practiced *voluntarily* through understanding of the law of giving and receiving, and in *faith* and *joy*. While it may be easier for a person to tithe when *required* to, it is better to do it *lovingly* and *freely* without coercion.

Every phase of your life becomes better, more harmonious and filled with right conditions and experiences when you tithe. You are cooperating with one of the oldest and most beneficial prosperity laws, that of gratitude. Your attitude of gratitude not only opens prosperity doors but keeps them open. Tithing is a practical way of saying "Thank You, God, for Your abundant supply." It is wise, therefore, to give your tithe lovingly and gratefully.

Tithing brings life improvement: "Since I have been tithing at least ten percent of my income, I have seen a change of attitude in our home. Everyone in our family, as well as my coworkers, seem to be more positive. We've been able to pay off a lot of bills, and I've been getting 'A's and 'B's at school. I feel more self confident and sure of myself. I continually remind myself that God is my Source and there are no limitations in my mind, body or financial affairs. Tithing is certainly working for me!"
- - *From Michigan*

When you tithe, does it always bring immediate increase?

Tithers usually discover that they begin to prosper when they invoke this prosperity law. Often increase comes rather suddenly.

Releasing tithe brings check: "For three months I had been expecting to receive a check for $90.00. Even though I was told several times that they were working on it, it didn't come. Then I released my tithe from some 'unexpected' income, and four days later the check was in my mail box! I have learned my lesson; never again will I withhold my tithe. I will give as it comes to me." - - *From Washington*

Prosperity cup overflows: "My cup is overflowing! So much good has come into my life since I began tithing, and using the Prayer-Treatment for 'unexpected' income, it is almost unbelievable. Yet, I know it is true and I gratefully accept my good. I have experienced healing of a long-standing illness, and have also sold property that had been for sale for a long time. My income has increased in a very nice way, too. Life is so much better and my whole family is happier." - - *From Nevada*

You can be sure that when you begin to tithe, *you will prosper more.* Even when it seems to take longer than you think it should, the 'gold dust' is gathering for you and will begin to settle soon!

When your prosperity may seem slow in coming or there are some financial challenges, these need not be a problem for tithers. They have the inner assurance that, regardless of appearances, all is well and they need only be patient because their richer good is on its way.

This is not meant to imply that because you tithe, you will never have financial challenges. You may have them, but because of the direct connection with the Source created by tithing, you need only to persist in faith, assured that everything will be okay as it surely will be.

Faithful tithers know: THEY HAVE A DIVINE CONNECTION WITH GOD, THE SOURCE. THEY ARE ALWAYS DIVINELY PROTECTED, AND EVEN IF SOME DOORS SEEM CLOSED, OR IF THERE ARE CHALLENGES, THINGS WILL WORK OUT AND THEY WILL BE BETTER OFF THAN BEFORE. THEIR PROSPERITY IS ASSURED.

They have good reason to know this. They know that they have something infinitely rich to rely upon. They have the assurance that all is well, and their comfort, supply and fulfillment are in good hands.

13

The
"Gratitude Attitude."

If you are looking for a way to open the coffers of universal riches, gratitude is one of the most effective. It is through the grateful heart that God pours His riches. Nothing much happens, except negative and undesirable things, to those with ungrateful attitudes.

A woman who had tried for years inquired as to why she didn't prosper. It was obvious to her counselor that she had a complaining, ungrateful attitude. When asked to listen to herself, and not liking what she heard, she decided to stop complaining and develop the "gratitude attitude." She was amazed at how her prosperity soon began to grow.

It pays to have the "Gratitude Attitude" --far more than a complaining one. The way to create the "Gratitude Attitude" is to be genuinely grateful for everything at the beginning of each day. Every morning when you awaken to a brand new day, give thanks to God for this new "Golden Opportunity"* to live, to do, and to be. Be grateful for all your blessings, especially, your loved ones. Give thanks for everything.

Even when you are going through some kind of challenge, give thanks for the growth it is allowing you to experience, and for the positive results that are coming to you in due time. Give thanks that Infinite Intelligence is working on what you are concerned with and bringing about the right outcome in Its own wonderful way.

Look about you and give thanks for what you see. If your surroundings are not as beautiful as you would like them to be, bless and give thanks for them, then do what you can to improve the situation. When you bless your surroundings, you set up a loving vibration that will make them better and bring more desirable circumstances. It is a wonderful way to practice the "Gratitude Attitude."

* "See the "Golden Opportunities" chapter in the author's book, *"Positively Alive!"*

A helpful practice is to make a list of at least ten things you have to be thankful for. Do this every day for a while. At the top, list the person whom you love the most, then follow with other people and things. Never say you don't have at least ten things to be grateful for. After spending some time on your list, you will be surprised at how long it is. Make your "grateful" list and give thanks for your many blessings.

A woman in Puerto Rico who has written several times, always tells me some of the things she is thankful for, most of them being her family and the good things that are happening to them. She expresses her gratitude for God's goodness to her and her loved ones. This lady is truly prosperous in gracious ways!

If life has been rather hard or if you have not prospered to the degree that you desire, try the "Gratitude Attitude" for at least thirty days. As you do so, look for things to be grateful for--even little, seemingly inconsequential things as well as the big important ones.

Let love well up within and be expressed in thanksgiving to God for being alive, as well as for all His blessings. If your blessings seem limited, you may increase them by being grateful for each one that you already have.

Another effective way to increase your good is to praise and appreciate. Dale Carnegie of *How to Win Friends and Influence People* fame, said to "speak up with praise and appreciation".

Granted, that is not always easy to do, especially if someone is difficult to get along with, you do not feel very loving toward that person, and life seems harder than it should be. However, when you practice loving and appreciating yourself and you realize that others are basically no different, it is easier to love them and speak with praise and appreciation. Praise and appreciation are expressions of the "Gratitude Attitude."

Try standing before a large mirror and talking to yourself, praising what a wonderful person you are and emphasizing that you are created in the image and likeness of God (Love) and therefore worth loving. You are divinely created. If you will do that every day for a while, you will gain a higher view of yourself as a divine being, worthy of being loved, and will find it easier to be loving. Praise and appreciation will come naturally to you. This practice will empower you to be divinely irresistible and attract to yourself, "unexpected" income in a variety of good forms.

How to Have "Unexpected" Income

Charles Fillmore, the co-founder of Unity School of Christianity, taught: *"Praise is the quality of mind that eulogizes the good; one of the avenues through which spirituality expresses."* and, *"Thanksgiving will keep the heart fresh, for true thanksgiving may be likened to rain falling upon ready soil, refreshing it and increasing its productiveness."*

There is a kind of mysticism about gratitude --of being genuinely thankful and letting it be expressed in words. For one thing, it frees the mind and eliminates old, critical, small thoughts and feelings. When that happens there is a free channel (your own thinking and feeling) through which God's vast good joyfully and abundantly flows. It is like unplugging a stopped-up drain, or unkinking a hose.

The result is a wonderful sense that all is well, regardless of appearances, and puts a light touch to all that you do. It further helps to create a wonderful flow of rich good in your life. You simply cannot measure the value of the "Gratitude Attitude."

From North Dakota: "I am so grateful that I was introduced to "unexpected" income at just the right time. However, at first it didn't work even though I faithfully used the Prayer-Treatment every day. There seemed to be some hang-up that I could not put my finger on.

"After giving it some thought, I realized that when I came to the part about being grateful in advance, I was just mouthing the words but didn't really mean them. As I sought for understanding, I learned that I had never actually developed an attitude of gratitude. I was thankful for some things, but did not give full, unconditional expression to thanksgiving--of being truly grateful for everything.

"I am happy to report, that soon after I began getting serious about being genuinely grateful (which was rather hard at first), something wonderful happened! I unexpectedly received a raise in pay, and was also named 'employee of the month.' My employer cited my obviously improved attitude and the ease with which I am now getting along with my co-workers. With the award came a small but very much appreciated bonus.

"I have experienced other unexpected income which was welcomed with open arms. It is fun to receive and I am much happier since getting involved with 'unexpected' income and changing my attitude to gratitude."

Receives financial bonus: "I am so thankful to report that I have received a generous, quite unexpected financial bonus! Thank you. I'm expecting more!" - - *From Nevada*

You can see that being genuinely grateful --speaking with praise and appreciation--is essential to your success in demonstrating "unexpected" income. It is an important ingredient in living life lovingly and successfully. The "Gratitude Attitude" lightens the load, and removes many of life's burdens. It will brighten your outlook and act in a mystical way to open the windows of heaven so that the Universe may pour out Its unlimited good for you.

It was Dr. Emmet Fox who said that thanksgiving is the royal road to demonstration because through the act of thanksgiving, you are not only confirming your complete faith in the power and goodness of God, but acknowledging the receipt of that good. Through praise and thanksgiving, all obstacles can be removed and your way straightened and made smooth.

It is wise to give thanks BEFORE receiving; it creates the consciousness of EXPECTANCY. Thus you create a unity with your heart's desires --and they are yours! In effect you are sending them an invitation to appear in your life.

It is also wise to give thanks AFTER receiving to complete the circuit which arranges for more happy financial "surprises" and other rich good to come to you. You have created an open and clear channel through which your desired increase loves to flow.

Speak up with praise and appreciation to other people, and especially thank God daily for His bounty now available and on its way to you. When you are genuinely grateful, you will hasten your good.

The "Gratitude Attitude" is the luxury vehicle that carries you along the royal road of *prosperous living*. It will carry you easily and far. You will be amazed at the happiness, health, companionship and financial blessings that will be demonstrated. Remember that the "Gratitude Attitude" is love in expression and love empowers you with divine irresistibility.

New clients come to her: "For the past several years I have enjoyed participating in 'unexpected' income which has been extremely helpful. This year an old client booked an appointment with me and paid me $100.00 for one hour of my time. In addition, I had two new clients who booked appointments for this week. Thanks, this really does work." - - *From California*

Gratitude opens prosperity doors: "Here is my testimonial of 'unexpected' income. It might not be considered income because it came in the form of service, but it could have cost a lot of money. I had wanted a check up for some time and was picturing money coming to pay for it. Out of the blue a call came that my husband and I could go through all necessary tests *absolutely free!*

"I attribute this to the fact that I expressed my thanks for receiving *before* I actually received. I expected to receive so I began being grateful in advance. We don't have to know *how* our good will come, only that God will manage it when we give thanks and let Him do it. Giving thanks in advance is trusting and believing in His goodness. I am a believer!" - - *From Oklahoma*

An enjoyable way to practice the "Gratitude Attitude" is to write "Thank you" notes to people. Obtain some of the nice cards that are now available, or just write notes of thanks on a piece of paper, and begin expressing gratitude today. The "Gratitude Attitude" will open doors for you and enrich your life in beautiful and prosperous ways.

When you think about it, you do have very much to be grateful for.

A Special word of Gratitude

I am especially thankful for the many friends whose love and tithes have helped me to establish the Golden Key Ministry, and who financially support its Prayer Ministry and newsletter. Thank you for all your past financial giving and for all that you continue to give.

- - John Wolcott Adams

14

More Reports of "Unexpected" Income

For many years, I have offered the Prayer-Treatment for "unexpected" income to the readers of my "Good News" newsletter. Usually the offer has been made early each summer so as to help people have a prosperous one. However, many participants continue using the Prayer-Treatment throughout the year.

As a result of their participation and inevitable success, I have received a large number of reports, enough possibly to fill a book by themselves. Although you have already read many others, here are additional reports to help you catch the spirit of this fun way to prosper.

Prayer-Treatment works quickly: "A friend shared the 'unexpected' income prayer-treatment with me and I used it three times daily. Within one week I unexpectedly received $300.00, and the following week I received another $300.00. I have received other smaller amounts, too. This thing works!" - - *From Alaska*

Receives gifts: "Someone sent me a gift of $50.00. People are always doing something nice for me. I live in a state of constant acceptance and am never really surprised. However, it is always great to receive and to share with others. I am joyful, happy and grateful because I know it is done unto us as we believe. Belief is acceptance." - - *From Colorado*

Sales increase: "Since getting involved in using the Prayer-treatment for 'unexpected' income, my sales have soared! I have also received many 'unexpected' gifts including one for over $500.00. I attribute my success to using the Prayer-Treatment and tithing. Before, it seemed like more struggle than fun, but no more. This is fun! Needless to say, I love the 'unexpected' income idea. I think it's great and I encourage others to get involved." - - *From Idaho*

How to Have "Unexpected" Income

Receives extra work: "My uncle unexpectedly sent $60.00 to me as a Christmas gift. When I went on vacation from my regular job, I was able to work at my weekend part time job for four nights. The Prayer-Treatment is working great for me!"   - - *From Missouri*

Financial prayers answered: "I have received $160.00 for doing yard work for a friend, and I have more work coming up. This came about since I began using the 'unexpected' income prayer-treatment."   - - *From Pennsylvania*

Receives larger pay: "My 'unexpected' income came through my employer. When I was hired full time, I thought I would be earning $1,500.00 per month. But when I received my first paycheck (for a half-month) it was for $800.00. Also, I have received other financial 'surprises'."
                                    - - *From Alabama*

Money keeps rolling in: "In the second half of last month, I received an 'unexpected' dividend of $90.00! To date I have received: $12.00; $13.00; $50.00; $30.00; $150.00; $40.00 and $20.00. I expect my next report to be even better. What a practical and fun way to increase my income!"
                                    - - *From Florida*

U.I. works in big way: "I am so glad I joined in 'unexpected' income. It is working for me in a big way. So far I have received over $650.00 in 'unexpected' income. I am looking forward to more prospering results for myself, my family and for everyone in this wonderful program."

- - From Quebec

Income increases: "Since I joined with you and everyone in the 'unexpected' income program, and have been cooperating with it as instructed, my income has increased substantially, not only from regular channels, but 'unexpected' ones too. This is evidently the result of no longer limiting my expectations but opening my mind to all possibilities and God's unlimited supply. I love it! My latest demonstration of 'unexpected' income was for $200.00! This is fun!" *- - From Ohio*

It pays to use the Prayer-Treatment: "Here is my 'unexpected' income report. I have received a total of $179.50 in 'unexpected' income in the past month. It sure pays to use the Prayer-Treatment daily and to keep open and receptive. Also, it is very helpful to tithe from all I receive, which I do faithfully" *- - From Michigan*

How to Have "Unexpected" Income

Blessings overflow: "I am very happy to report the wonderful blessings coming into my life. My son has found good employment, and my husband's family was able to come for a visit after several years. We were unexpectedly given $1,000.00! My daughter received financial help at the University. I thank God for everything every day! Thank you for the Prayer-Treatment for 'unexpected' income. It is wonderful and works beautifully." - - *From Puerto Rico*

Receives unexpected refund: "I had left a deposit on an item at a department store several months ago. When I changed my mind and purchased the item at another store I thought I would not get my deposit back. However, a few days ago after I had begun using the Prayer-Treatment for 'unexpected' income, there was a refund check in my mail box! It works!" - - *From New York*

Finds unexpected funds: "After joining the 'unexpected' income program, I have twice found unexpected funds in my checking account. The first time, I had no food when I discovered I had $90.00 in the account. The next week I found another $110.00. Since then my income has improved substantially due to finding a good job. I know that my involvement in 'unexpected' income helped me in that, too. It really works." - - *From Oregon*

Receives more than expected: "Because of a slight relapse after surgery, my doctor extended my disability two more weeks. However, I was able to return to work earlier than I thought I would. When I received my disability check, it was for $75.00 more than expected. I have healed quickly and completely, my health is good, and I think that my involvement with 'unexpected' income has something to do with that. I believe it helps to make life easier and more enjoyable!"   - - *From California*

"Unexpected" income passes test: "After receiving the 'unexpected' income information, I was at least a little skeptical but decided to put it to the test. I joined in and began to use the Prayer-Treatment, declaring the affirmations a couple of times each day. I also decided to open my mind to new channels although I couldn't see how more money could come to me. But it did!

"I am happy to report that it works! So far I have received over $300.00 from totally unexpected sources that I had never before considered. (One was the state lottery!) 'Unexpected' income has passed the test. I continue to use the Prayer-Treatment daily and urge others to use it too. I appreciate your making this available for me and so many others. Thanks!"   - - *From Illinois*

How to Have "Unexpected" Income

Release of tithe brings increase "For over three months I had been expecting to receive a check for a sizeable amount. I was told it was being worked on but it still did not come. I was using the Prayer-Treatment for 'unexpected' income and had received small financial blessings but not that check!

"Then I remembered that I had not released my tithe from other 'unexpected' income that I had received and immediately sent my tithe. Three days later, the check was in my mail box! I have learned my lesson! I am continuing to declare the Prayer-Treatment and to tithe!"
- - *From California*

"Unexpected" income works for her: "I am happy to report that I have received some additional unexpected income, from another birthday gift and from a most unexpected source who wished to pay for items given to her some time ago. Another is a totally unexpected refund on an unsatisfactory purchase. I am so happy to be included daily in everyone's Prayer-Treatment. Thanks for a such a great idea. You are very much appreciated! - - *From Washington, D. C.*

"Unexpected" income brings healing: "It is amazing how working with the 'unexpected' income affirmations (Prayer-Treatment) has helped me get well. Since opening my mind to more prosperity an illness has cleared up, saving me many dollars in doctor and other medical bills. It is great to be prosperous in health again. And I have received some small monetary gifts which were unexpected but gratefully accepted! Focusing on 'unexpected' income helped me to get my mind off of the negative and onto the positive--it's the only way to go! It is my pleasure to tithe from all that I receive." - - *From Alabama*

Gets part time job: "I have been praying faithfully and using the Prayer-Treatment for 'unexpected' income. Only six days later I got the job I wanted, and also sold an old picture for $40.00. This is exciting! I'm ready for more 'unexpected' income!" - - *From New York*

Receives unexpected gift: "I have received 'unexpected' income for the Christmas holidays. I had joined in using the Prayer-Treatment for 'unexpected' income a few months ago and it worked in small ways. I made a lateral career change which did not include a pay raise. This Christmas was my first as the new secretary for a management staff who all chipped in and gave me a really nice financial gift which was totally unexpected but very much appreciated."

- - *From New York*

Mental attitude improves: "Many thanks for helping me improve my mental attitude. I attribute it to my involvement in using the Prayer-Treatment for 'unexpected' income. Previously my attitude was one of confusion and frustration, and now it is one of positive expectancy. I don't know why the Prayer-Treatment has worked that way, but it has and some wonderful things have happened in my life because of my new attitude and my affirming of the Prayer-Treatment each day.

"One day I visited a temporary employment agency where there were positive thoughts taped on the walls. The owner quickly found a job where I could use my education and skills. It paid more money than I had believed I could get from that type of work. I have received some gifts of money and other things, too. It is wonderful how the Prayer-Treatment works. I don't know why it does--it just does!" - - *From Georgia*

Business bonus: "I have just received a nice business bonus in the amount of $300.00 which was quite unexpected."   - - *From Louisiana*

Receives $$$ gift: "Yesterday, I received a gift of $80.00.   The Prayer-Treatment for 'unexpected' income surely works! I urge everyone to get involved in this wonderful, fun way to increase their prosperity." - - *From Pennsylvania*

Receives salary increase and bonus check: "Here is my 'unexpected' income report.   A promotion at work brought me a $100.00 per month increase in my salary plus an opportunity to earn bonuses. I just received an unexpected bonus check in the amount of $250.00. I am expecting more 'unexpected' income!"
- - *From California*

"Unexpected" Income works for her: "Over and over I have declared the 'unexpected' income affirmations which I have taped up on my refrigerator. Two weeks ago I had an especially good week with my Mary Kay business and made some unexpectedly good sales. That came after I made a commitment to tithe at least 10% of all I receive. U. I. and tithing are working for me."
- - *From California*

"Unexpected" income works for him: "Since joining with you and everyone in using the Prayer-Treatment for 'unexpected' income, some very interesting things have happened to me. I have received a Texas-size financial blessing. Starting off slowly with rather small demonstrations of 'unexpected' income, I unexpectedly sold a piece of property I had tried to sell for years. Selling it at this time brought me a lot more money than it would have earlier.

"You have made a believer out of me and I also recommend this to my friends. Everyone should get involved in using the Prayer-Treatment and begin expecting 'unexpected' income!"

- - *From Texas*

Just as these people have demonstrated the efficacy of the Prayer-Treatment for "unexpected" income, so can you. In the following chapter you will find more ideas to help you increase your prosperity through daily use of the Prayer-Treatment for "unexpected" income.

"All things are possible to him who believes."

- - Mark 11: 23

15

For Your Success!

Following are several important things to remember for success in demonstrating "unexpected" income:

1. Faith. Believe what you are doing is worthwhile and IS bringing the desired results. Put your faith to work by using the Prayer-Treatment every day for yourself and fellow "unexpected" income participants. Combined positive prayer power is an important key to everyone's success.

Believe that you receive and believe that everyone else is prospering too. In faith, accept the expected good, and keep open and receptive to every possibility. You never know where or how your rich good is going to show up in your life! So believe and receive!

123

2. Giving. "Unexpected" income is not only about receiving, but about the giving of your money to "prime the pump", so-to-speak, and it is also more than that. It is the giving of your talents, abilities, time and energy in loving service to others, as well as the giving of your substance.

The more you give the more you receive; that is why tithing is so highly recommended as explained in Chapter Twelve. Tithing is your "connecting link" with God, the Source. Tithing, is your 'golden key' to success and abundance, through your participation in "unexpected" income.

Look for ways and opportunities to bless others, to lend a helping hand even when you receive no apparent remuneration. All that you give in loving service and material ways accumulates, therefore do not be surprised when down the road a rather sudden "unexpected" financial blessing is dumped in your lap. It happens all the time and there is no reason why it won't happen to you.

3. The Golden Rule. Using the Prayer-Treatment for "unexpected" income for yourself, plus making sure you include everyone else, is practicing the Golden Rule. Doing to others what you would like others to do to you is another way of expressing love. Love is the real name of the game!

Every time you come to the part about knowing that all the participants are being blessed, too, let your thought go out to them. Send them a silent beam of love. You cannot imagine how powerful it is. Don't be surprised when you feel it coming back to you--magnified and multiplied!

4. Easy does it. It is essential, if you really desire to demonstrate "unexpected" income, that you make a commitment to faithfully affirm the Prayer-Treatment every day. Take this book in hand, open, and read the Prayer-Treatment. Make it a regular practice early in the day. It is often helpful to include it in your daily prayer time. After all, it is a wonderful prayer and has immense power to make a prospering difference in your life, and in the lives of loved ones and others.

Remember: Easy does it, so let Easy do it! As Ralph Waldo Emerson said, "Get your bloated nothingness out of the way and let God do the work." There is simply no way that you can *make* "unexpected" income or anything else come to you. So don't *try*--LET, relax and have fun! Keep it light. If your demonstration seems delayed, you may be trying too hard so take it easy. Lighten up and *let* it happen. It does so more quickly with *you* out of the way.

Do not be anxious because anxiety is fear. Fear will not produce the good that you desire. Allow yourself to have a lightheartedness about this activity. Don't try to *make* something happen; that is not your job. Your role is to declare the Prayer-Treatment each day, then let it go in the assurance that you have done your work, and that's good enough for today. Relax and let Infinite Intelligence* do the work. It is, so take it easy. Let go and let it happen. When you do you *will* receive "unexpected" Income.

*For more on letting Infinite Intelligence do the work, please see the author's book, "Thirty Days to a Better Life."

5. Keep your talk positive. Do not use the Prayer-Treatment and then engage in negative or pessimistic chatter. Refrain from acting as though it is not true. Keep your talk positive and in harmony with the Prayer-Treatment. Think, speak and act as though you sincerely believe in what you declare when you use the Prayer-Treatment.

If you do not demonstrate "unexpected" income right away, do not be dismayed. Keep on using the Prayer-Treatment. It will help to lift your faith to a higher level. Speak as though you have already received and more is on the way; act in the same way. You will be surprised how this helps to speed your demonstration. Be optimistic. After all, you are doing something positive to bring wonderful financial increase. Think and speak positively. Relax, let go, accept and enjoy!

"Keep your vision uplifted today. Make a determined effort to look for the good, to be happy and to practice the presence of God within and around you."

From: "Positively Alive!"

In Conclusion . . .

Now that you have read this book through, it is time to get to work. Turn back to the Prayer-Treatment for "unexpected" income on pages 20 and 21. You have already read it but read it again, this time audibly. As explained earlier, it is better to speak these words aloud. If you cannot be alone, and someone else might object or be offended, do it silently. Sometimes you may want to retreat to another room where you can be by yourself.

When you speak the words again, you are starting the action. Keep on using the Prayer-Treatment each day as you open your mind to "unexpected" financial and other exciting "surprises."

Invite family members to join with you in the "unexpected" income activity. It's a wonderful way for the whole family to share in the benefits of "unexpected" income!

Never say it doesn't work. There is plenty of proof in this book that it does. It will work for you when you utilize it in faith, and to the degree that you really want and can allow yourself to accept.

I love to receive reports from readers who are participating in this fun way to prosper. I'll be glad to receive yours, too.

If you are declaring the Prayer-Treatment as prescribed, you *WILL* demonstrate "unexpected" income. More than that, you will cause an ever-increasing stream of financial and other blessings to flow for you. When your increases come, as they surely will, please write and let me share in your joy.

God is blessing you right now with a wonderful new life--a life filled with His richest good, plenty of love, happiness and all that is worth having. *Go for it with all your heart!*

John Wolcott Adams
P.O. Box 13356
Scottsdale, AZ 85267-3356
USA

How to Have "Unexpected" Income

Enjoy all of the author's books.

Buy them where you purchased this book, or use this form to order directly from the author. Mail to: Golden Key Minstry-Unity, P. O. Box 13356, Scottsdale, AZ 85267.

Please send to me, the following books by John Wolcott Adams: *(Indicate the quantity of each book you desire.)*

_____ *Positively Alive!* @ $8.95
Empowers you for positive daily living.

_____ *Power Words for Prosperous Living!* @ $6.95
Reveals the prospering power of your words.

_____ *BE What You Are: LOVE* @ $6.95
Helps you live life lovingly, free, and be what you really are..

_____ *How to Have "Unexpected" Income!* @ $6.95
A powerhouse of prospering energy. Numerous testimonials!

_____ *Thirty Days To A Better Life* @ $3.95
Yes! Your life *can* be better in just thirty days!

_____ *Million Dollar bill* (10" X 17") @ $5.00

(Prices are in U.S. dollars and include postage except Canada & Overseas. Please add $1.00 to each price.)

Please put me on your mailing list to receive: *Upward Quest* Newsletter, *a Treasure of Ideas promoting a Happy, Peaceful, Prosperous, Unlimited Way of Life.* ☐

Name _____

Address_____

City, State, ZIP+4_____

Total amount enclosed: $_____

Golden Key Ministry-Unity is a worldwide prayer ministry by mail and welcomes prayer requests for all good desires. Use the back of this sheet for your prayer request.

e-mail: gkm@amug.org